Dropping In On...

BRAZIL

David C. King

A Geography Series

ROURKE BOOK COMPANY, INC.
VERO BEACH, FLORIDA 32964

A Blackbirch Graphics book.
Series Editor: Tanya Lee Stone

Printed in the United States of America.

Library of Congress Cataloging-in-Publication Data

King, David C.
    Brazil / David C. King
        p.   cm. — (Dropping in on)
    Includes index.
    ISBN 1-55916-082-9
    1. Brazil—Description and travel—Juvenile literature. [1. Brazil—Description and travel.]
I. Title. II. Series.
    F2517.K56   1995
    918.104'64—dc20   94-37253
                                                CIP
                                                AC

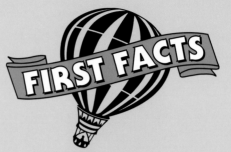

Brazil

Official Name: Federative Republic of Brazil

Area: 3,286,470 square miles

Population: 158,739,000

Capital: Brasília

Largest City: São Paulo

Highest Elevation: Pico da Neblina (9,889 feet)

Official Language: Portuguese

Major Religion: Roman Catholic

Money: Cruzeiro

Form of Government: Federal Republic

Flag:

TABLE OF CONTENTS

Our Blue Ball—The Earth

The Earth can be divided into two hemispheres. The word hemisphere means "half a ball"—in this case, the ball is the Earth.

The equator is an imaginary line that runs around the middle of the Earth. It separates the Northern Hemisphere from the Southern Hemisphere. North America—where Canada, the United States, and Mexico are located—is in the Northern Hemisphere.

The Southern Hemisphere

When the South Pole is tilted toward the sun, the sun's most powerful rays strike the southern half of the Earth and less sunshine hits the Northern Hemisphere. That is when people in the Southern Hemisphere enjoy summer. When the

South Pole is tilted away from the sun, and the Northern Hemisphere receives the most sunshine, the seasons reverse. Then winter comes to the Southern Hemisphere. The seasons in the Southern Hemisphere and the Northern Hemisphere are always opposite. Most of Brazil is in the Southern Hemisphere.

Get Ready for Brazil

Are you ready to take a trip? Hop into your hot-air balloon and let's go!

You are about to drop in on a country that is larger than the United States. Most of Brazil is in the Southern Hemisphere. Brazil is bordered by the Atlantic Ocean. More than 158 million people live here.

The equator runs through Brazil, which means the country has warm to hot temperatures all through the year. Almost half of the country is covered by the Amazon rainforest. The Amazon is the world's largest rainforest.

Stop 1: Salvador

For our first stop, we'll drop in on the city of Salvador. Salvador is perched on a high cliff overlooking the Atlantic Ocean. The best way to get up and down the cliff is to ride one of the city's big elevators.

As you walk along the streets of Salvador, you will see many beautiful churches and cathedrals. Some of them are even decorated with gold! Now and then, a truck will move slowly along a street. From the back of the truck, musicians called *trios electricos* play lively music.

Because of the warm weather, people spend much of their time on the beaches. Some Salvadorans swim or sunbathe. Others collect shellfish. Behind the beaches, there are freshwater ponds called lagoons. People fish in the lagoons and also use them to wash clothes.

*Next, let's travel **southwest** along the Atlantic coast to Rio de Janeiro.*

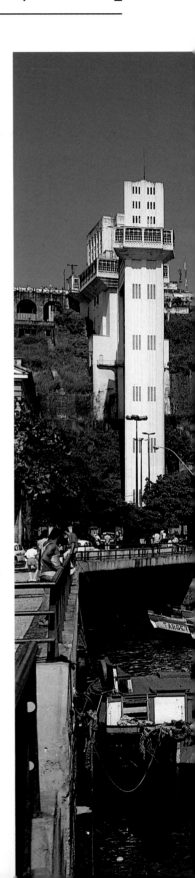

The city of Salvador was built
on a cliff facing the harbor.

Atlantic Ocean

Amazon River

Salvador
1

Pacific
Ocean

N
W — E
S

Tall mountains tower over Rio de Janeiro's Botafogo Bay.

Stop 2: Rio de Janeiro

Rio de Janeiro is one of the most beautiful cities in the world. As our hot-air balloon floats above the bay, you can see miles of white sand beaches. A mountain called Sugar Loaf rises up out of the blue water of the bay. Behind the city, other mountains tower above the buildings.

More than 9 million people live in the city that many people call "Rio" for short. Rio is an important seaport, visited by ships from many countries. The city is also a center for making shoes and clothing.

Most of all, Rio is famous for two things—beaches and Carnaval. The beaches are always busy. People sunbathe, swim, fish, and play soccer or volleyball. Schoolchildren even bring their homework to the beach. The beaches are also a marketplace. You can buy food, jewelry, balloons, and ice cream from beach vendors.

People on a colorful float entertain the crowd during a Carnaval parade.

Carnaval is Rio's exciting celebration. It is held each year for 5 days ending on Ash Wednesday. Weeks before Carnaval begins, the air is filled with the sound of music, especially for a dance called the *samba*. Thousands of people belong to *samba* clubs. They meet every weekend to get ready for Carnaval, making costumes and floats for the parade and practicing their dances.

The Carnaval parade begins on Sunday evening and ends on Monday afternoon. Crowds line the streets as 80,000 club members march, sing, and dance. Prizes are given for the best floats, costumes, and dancers. Tourists from all over the world enjoy Carnaval.

Festival Time in Brazil

Every city and town in Brazil celebrates Carnaval. There are also many other festivals during the year. Some of them are religious celebrations. In one town, you might see people march through the streets carrying flowers and lanterns or candles. The procession ends with a washing of the town church. Other festivals are dedicated to New Year's. In fishing villages, the New Year's festivals are held to pray for a good year of fishing.

Every festival and Carnaval means plenty of loud and lively Brazilian music. At Carnaval time, a *samba* band may have as many as 800 drummers—all playing at once!

Samba *dancers twirl to the music at Carnaval time.*

Now we'll head **southwest** to São Paulo.

Stop 3: São Paulo

São Paulo is located a few miles inland from the ocean. The city is built on a plateau that is more than 2,000 feet above sea level.

More than 15 million people live in the São Paulo area. It is the largest city in Brazil. São Paulo has many modern buildings and gleaming skyscrapers. Almost half of Brazil's factories are located in or near the city. Trucks and trains carry goods to the nearby seaport. Brazil produces more coffee and oranges than any other country in the world.

A Brazilian man sifts coffee beans.

São Paulo, with its crowded streets, is one of the largest cities in the world.

São Paulo is famous for its restaurants. For lunch, you might try a favorite Brazilian sandwich called the *bauru*. The *bauru* has beef, tomato, and a mixture of melted cheeses. You can also stop at a *suco bar* for a thick fruit-juice drink.

Now let's travel **southwest** *again to the Pampas and meet Brazil's cowboys.*

Stop 4: The Pampas

A gaucho dressed in traditional clothing.

As we travel toward the southern part of Brazil, we come to an area of rolling grassland called the Pampas. On the Pampas, you can watch the Brazilian cowboys called *gauchos*. Like American cowboys, *gauchos* are proud of their skill on horseback. With their trained horses, they drive herds of cattle to market or to fresh pasture. When they are on the trail, the *gauchos* sleep under the stars.

Gauchos wear baggy pants called *bombachas* and colorful shirts. Leather aprons protect their legs.

Near the Pampas is a spot named Iguaçu Falls. At the Falls, more than 30 rivers and streams plunge down a 230-foot cliff. There are 275 waterfalls at Iguaçu.

Next, we will travel **northeast** *to Brasília, the capital of Brazil.*

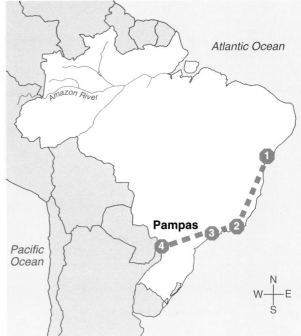

Many streams and rivers rush together to form the majestic Iguaçu Falls.

Stop 5: Brasília

Brasília is one of the newest cities in the world. From the air, you can see that the city is laid out in the shape of an airplane. Government buildings are located in the body shape of the plane. Homes and hotels are in the 2 curved wings.

Brasília is located far inland from the Atlantic coast in Brazil's western frontier. Before 1960, few people lived in this region. The government

These unique modern structures house Brazil's government offices.

decided to move the nation's capital from Rio de Janeiro to this region. The building of Brasília began in 1957 and it became the new capital just 3 years later.

Some of the government offices in Brasília are in tall towers. Others are located in a low, round building that looks like a giant saucer. The city faces a human-made lake. Nearby, the National Park of Brazil has natural swimming pools. You can see many of Brazil's wild animals in the park.

LET'S TAKE TIME OUT

Growing Up in Brazil

Brazilian children start school when they are 7 years old. For the next 7 years, they learn to read and write in Portuguese, the language of Brazil. They also study math, science, and history.

The seasons in the Southern Hemisphere are opposite those north of the equator. Because of this, Brazilian students have their summer vacation in December and January.

Nearly half the children leave school after the fourth grade. They go to work in order to earn money for their families. Some kids work as household servants. Others become street vendors. They sell newspapers, food, or clothing on street corners. Many Brazilian boys, called *guia*, work as guides for tourists. Even when they have jobs, Brazilians can continue their education. They can go to special evening schools. Other courses are given on the radio or on television.

Brazilian kids spend their free time on the beaches or in parks. Soccer is their favorite game, and every boy and girl has a favorite team. There are more than 20,000 soccer teams in Brazil.

Opposite: Brazilian children can spend their free time playing outside year-round, due to the warm climate.

Next, *let's head* **northwest** *to Manaus in the Amazon rainforest.*

Stop 6: Manaus

This stop takes us deep into the Amazon rainforest. The city of Manaus is located near a spot where 2 rivers come together to join the Amazon River. The Amazon is the mightiest river in the world. It is 4,000 miles long and it carries more water to the sea than any other river. Along the river bank, you might see manatees, river otters, or porpoises swimming in the water. Ocean-going ships can sail more than 2,000 miles upriver.

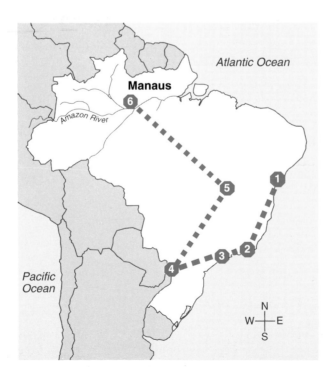

The Rio Negro is one of the branches, or tributaries, that form the Amazon. Inset: The beautiful Manaus opera house was built in 1896.

Manaus is near the equator. The weather is hot and humid all year. The months from January to June are the rainy season. During these months, there is a rain shower almost every day.

One hundred years ago, Manaus was the center of Brazil's rubber industry. Rubber trees in the rainforest were tapped for their gooey sap called latex. The latex was then used to make rubber for tires, boots, rubber balls, and many other items.

In Manaus, you may want to visit the famous opera house, built in the nineteenth century. Operas and ballets are performed there throughout the year.

The Amazon Rainforest

Every day, several boats leave Manaus for trips into the rainforest. Tourists can take a day cruise or longer trips that last a week or more.

As the boat cruises slowly upriver, everyone looks for wildlife. You can see spider monkeys and howler monkeys high in the trees. The monkeys share the treetops with colorful birds, including parrots, toucans, and macaws. There are anteaters,

jaguars, turtles, alligators, and tapirs. More than 200 kinds of snakes live in the Amazon rainforest and there are more than 1,800 different kinds of butterflies, some as large as a person's hand.

The toucan (top left), the spider monkey (bottom left), and the jaguar (above) are some of the many kinds of animals that make their home in the Amazon rainforest.

The Amazon rainforest covers almost half of Brazil. The trees are so thick that almost no sunlight reaches the ground. More than 180 Indian tribes live in this region. Most of Brazil's Indians live in small

A young Kaipo Indian boy is dressed in special paint and clothing for a tribal ceremony.

groups of less than 200 people. They clear a small part of the rainforest for their villages and crops. Several families live together in one large house called a *maloca*. They sleep in hammocks. Hammocks were invented by Brazilian Indians!

Many of the tribes have small farm plots where they grow manioc. Manioc is a root that is ground into flour. Tapioca is also made from manioc. Some Indian tribes still live by hunting and fishing, as their ancestors have done for centuries. Others have moved into cities to find jobs.

*We'll now travel **east** to Belém, our last stop.*

Fishermen sell their fresh catch in an open-air market in Belém.

Stop 7: Belém

Belém is the largest port on the Amazon River. Near Belém, the Amazon divides into many branches in its rush to the Atlantic Ocean.

Belém is one of the rainiest cities in the world. It has a famous market on the riverfront. Here you can watch fishing boats unload their catch. There are more than 1,500 kinds of fish in the Amazon. Scientists have not even found names for all of them yet. One fish, called the mura, is as big as a human. Other fishes have unusual shapes. You might see the butterfly fish, the leaf fish, or one called the window cleaner fish.

Restaurants in Belém are well known for their seafood. A favorite dish is *vatapá*. This is a stew made of fish, shrimp, ginger, and coconut milk. You can also buy different kinds of fruit that are found only in the Amazon rainforest.

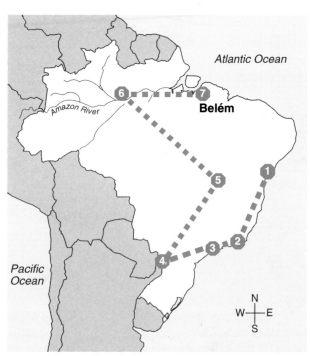

Now it's time to set sail for home. When you return, you can think back on the wonderful adventure you had in Brazil.

Glossary

Carnaval A Brazilian holiday and festival that lasts for 5 days, ending on Ash Wednesday.

gaucho A Brazilian cowboy.

lagoon A pond located near an ocean.

maloca A common house shared by several families in a Brazilian Indian village.

manioc A root grown in the Amazon rainforest and used to make flour or tapioca.

plateau A flat area of land that is higher than sea level.

rainforest A thick evergreen forest located in hot, wet tropical regions, with rainfall of at least 100 inches per year.

samba Brazilian dance music; the most popular form of music in Brazil.

Further Reading

Bailey, Donna and Sproule, Anna. *Brazil.* Madison, NJ: Raintree Steck-Vaughn, 1990.

Bennett, Olivia. *Family in Brazil.* Minneapolis, MN: Lerner, 1984.

Cobb, Vicki. *This Place is Wet.* New York: Walker and Company, 1989.

Jacobsen, Ken. *Brazil.* Chicago: Childrens Press, 1990.

Lewington, Anna. *Antonio's Rain Forest.* Minneapolis, MN: Carolrhoda Books, 1993.

Waterlow, Julia. *Brazil.* New York: Bookwright, 1992.

Index

Acknowledgments and Photo Credits
Cover and page 22: ©Suzanne L. Murphy/DDB Stock Photo; pp. 4, 5–6: National
Aeronautics and Space Administration; pp. 10–11, 28: ©Fridmar Damm/Leo de Wys, Inc.;
p. 12: ©Will and Deni McIntyre/Photo Researchers, Inc.; p. 14: ©Fernando Natalici; p. 15:
©Gamba/Sipa/Leo de Wys, Inc.; p. 16: ©John Moss/Photo Researchers, Inc.; p. 17: ©Joac
Messerschmidt/Leo de Wys, Inc.; p. 18: ©Carlos Goldin/DDB Stock Photo; pp. 18–19:
©Michael Everett/DDB Stock Photo; pp. 20–21: ©George Holton/Photo Researchers, Inc.;
pp. 24–25: ©Robert Fried/DDB Stock Photo; p. 25 (inset): ©Porterfield/Chickering/Photo
Researchers, Inc.; p. 26 (top left): ©François Gohier/Photo Researchers, Inc.; p. 26 (bottom
left): ©Dudu Cavalcanti/DDB Stock Photo; p. 26 (right): ©Simon/Photo Researchers, Inc.;
p. 27: ©Nair Benedicto/DDB Stock Photo.

Maps by Blackbirch Graphics, Inc.